Visual CSS Grid

Visual CSS Grid

Oluwatobi Sofela

CODESWEETLY

First published by CodeSweetly 2023

VISUAL CSS GRID

Front Cover Floral Pattern Illustrator: Satheesh Sankaran

First edition. May 4, 2023.

www.codesweetly.com

Contents

Contents

Grid Container vs. Grid Item

A grid container (the large area below) is an HTML element whose display property's value is grid or inline-grid. Grid items (the smaller boxes within the large container) are the direct children of a grid container.

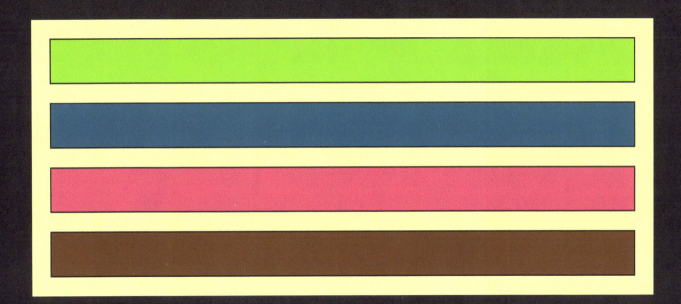

🐦 @oluwatobiss

📷 @codesweetly

🌐 codesweetly.com

justify-content

justify-content: start

start positions the grid container's columns with its row-start edge.

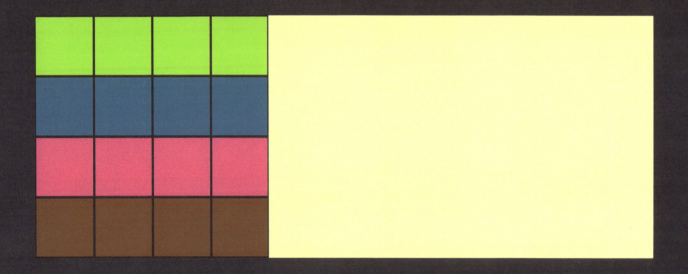

justify-content: center

center positions the grid container's columns to the center of the grid's row axis.

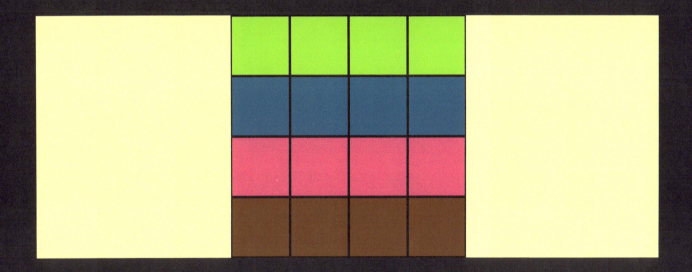

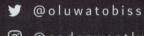
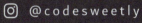

justify-content: end

end positions a grid container's columns with its row-end edge.

justify-content: space-between

space-between creates even spacing between each pair of columns between the first and last grid column

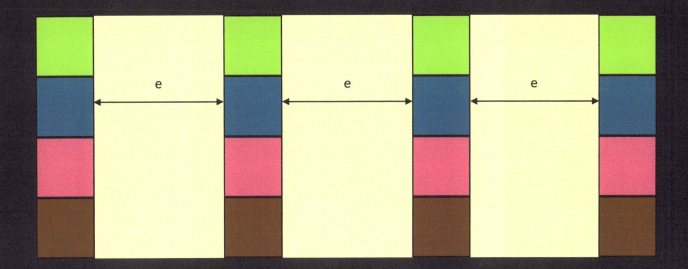

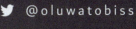

justify-content: space-around

space-around assigns equal spacing to each side of a grid container's columns.

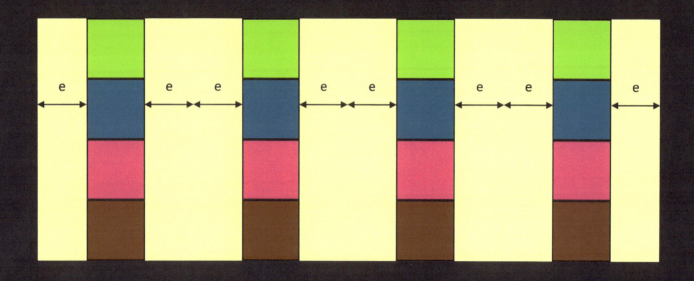

justify-content: space-evenly

space-evenly assigns even spacing to both ends of a grid container and between its columns.

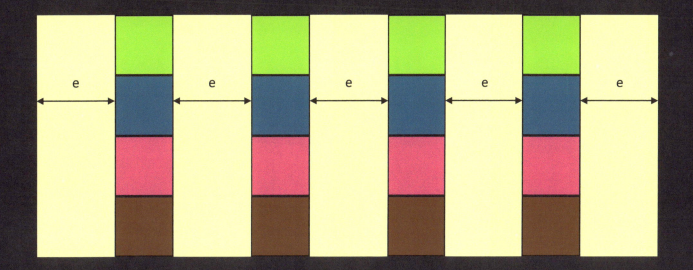

justify-items

justify-items: stretch

stretch stretches a grid container's items to fill their individual cells' row (inline) axis.

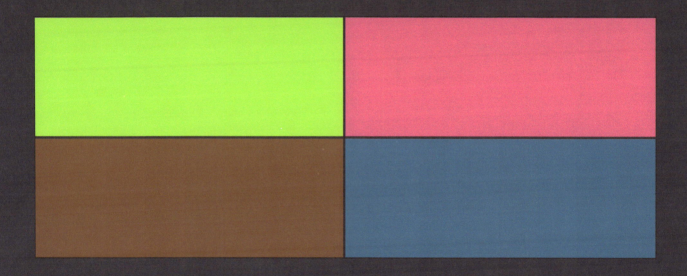

justify-items: start

start positions a grid container's items with the row-start edge of their individual cells' row axis.

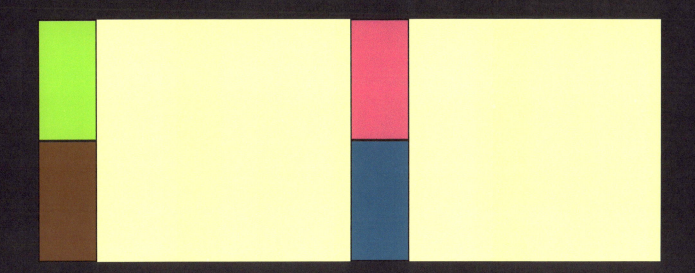

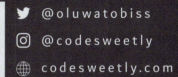
21

justify-items: center

center positions a grid container's items to the center of their individual cells' row axis.

justify-items: end

end positions a grid container's items with the row-end edge of their individual cells' row axis.

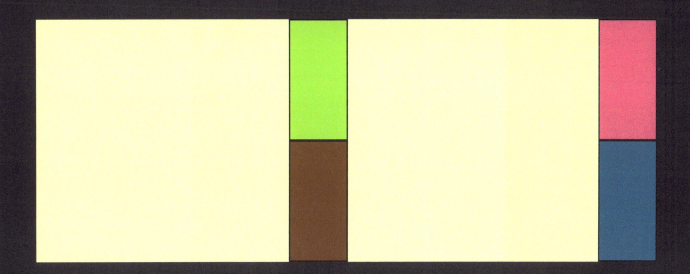

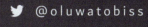
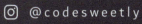
23

align-content

align-content: stretch

stretch stretches the grid container's rows to fill the grid's cross-axis.

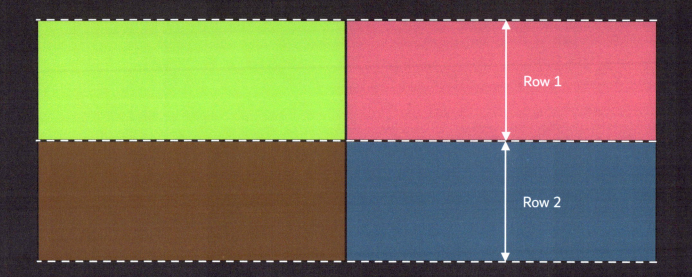

align-content: start

start aligns a grid container's rows with the column-start edge of the grid's column axis.

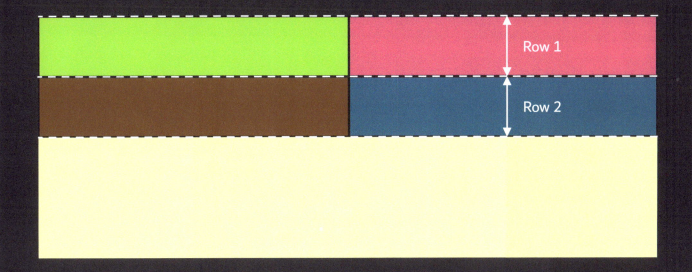

align-content: center

center aligns a grid container's rows to the center of the grid's column axis.

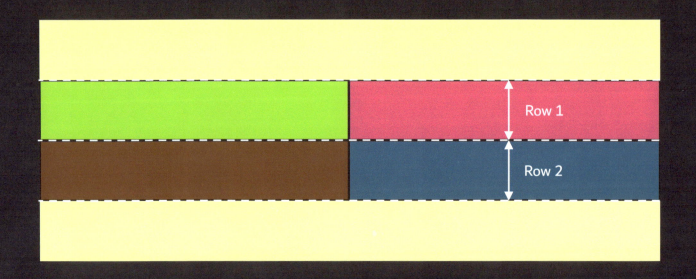

align-content: end

end aligns a grid container's rows with the column-end edge of the grid's column axis.

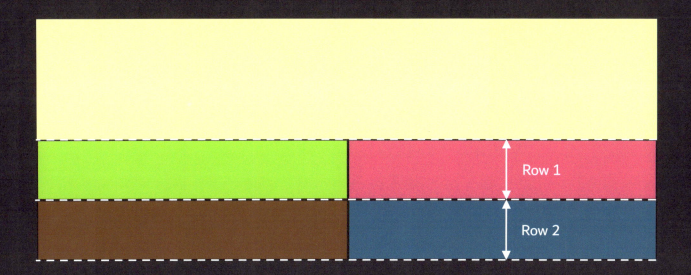

align-content: space-between

space-between creates even spacing between each pair of rows between the first and last grid row

align-content: space-around

space-around assigns equal spacing to each side of a grid container's rows.

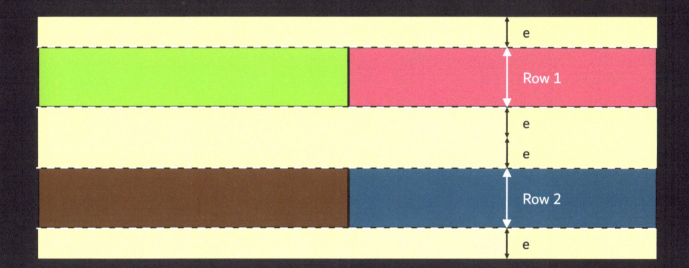

align-content: space-evenly

space-evenly assigns even spacing to both ends of a grid container and between its rows.

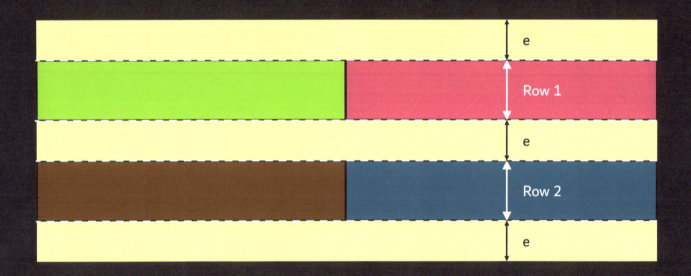

align-items

align-items: stretch

stretch stretches the grid container's items to fill their individual cells' column (block) axis.

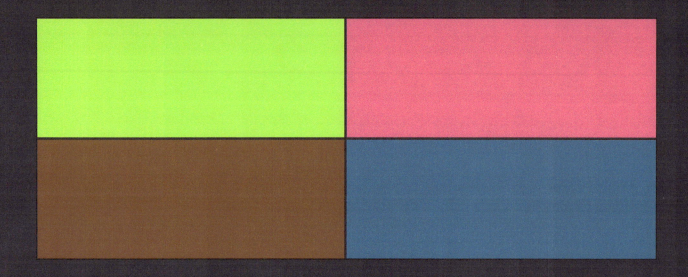

align-items: start

start aligns a grid container's items with the column-start edge of their individual cells' column axis.

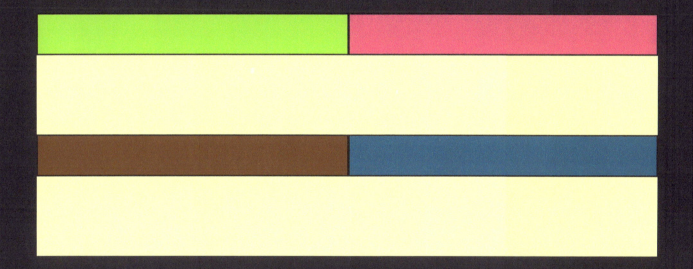

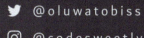

align-items: center

center aligns a grid container's items to the center of their individual cells' column axis.

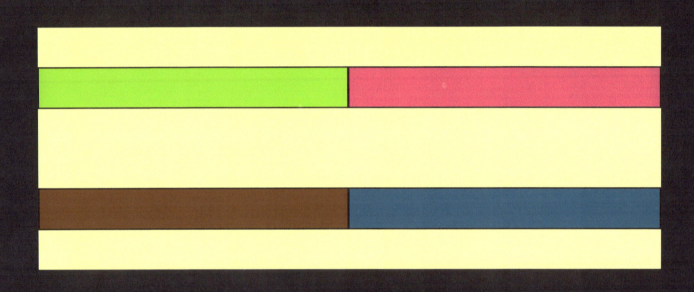

align-items: end

end aligns a grid container's items with the column-end edge of their individual cells' column axis.

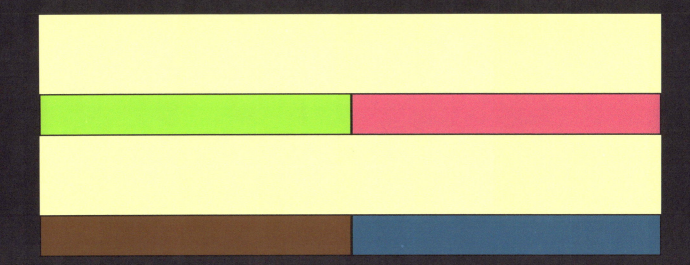

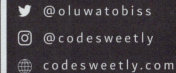

justify-self

justify-self: stretch

stretch stretches the selected grid item to fill its cell's row (inline) axis.

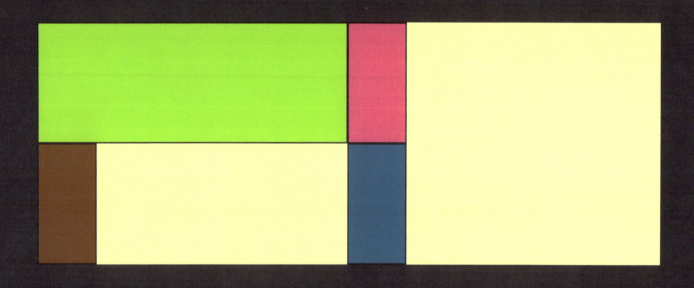

justify-self: start

start positions the selected grid item with the row-start edge of its cell's row axis.

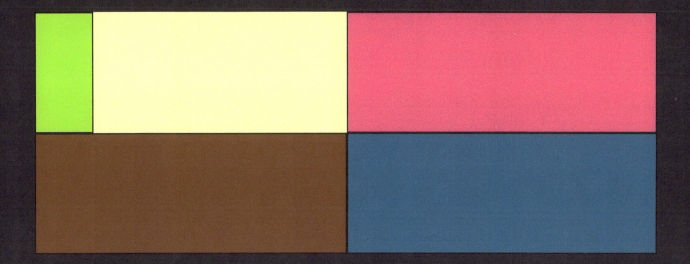

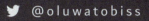
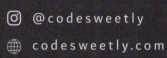

justify-self: center

center positions the selected grid item to the center of its cell's row axis.

justify-self: end

end positions the selected grid item with the row-end edge of its cell's row axis.

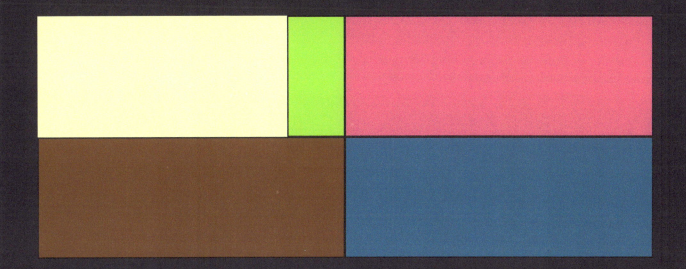

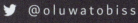

align-self

align-self: stretch

stretch stretches the selected grid item to fill its cell's column (block) axis.

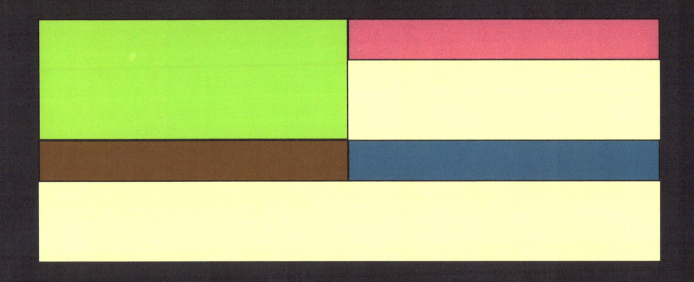

align-self:start

start aligns the selected grid item with the column-start edge of its cell's column axis.

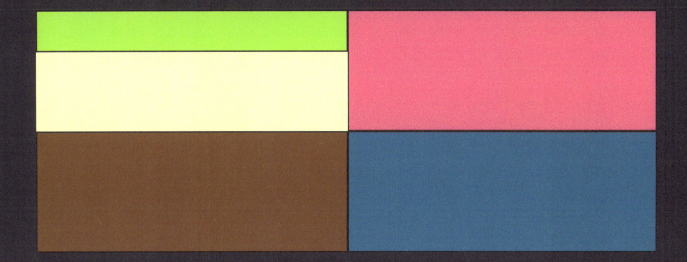

align-self: center

center aligns the selected grid item to the center of its cell's column axis.

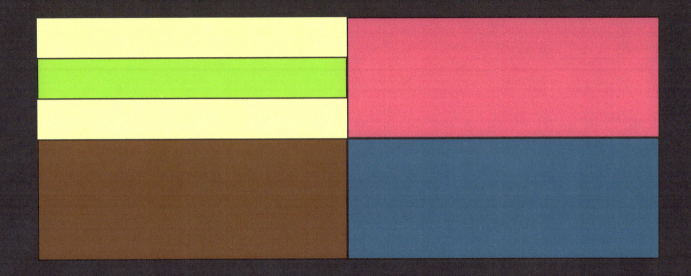

align-self:end

end aligns the selected grid item with the column-end edge of its cell's column axis.

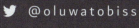
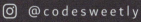

CSS Grid Lines

CSS grid lines are the lines browsers create on a grid container when you define the grid-template-columns or grid-template-rows property.

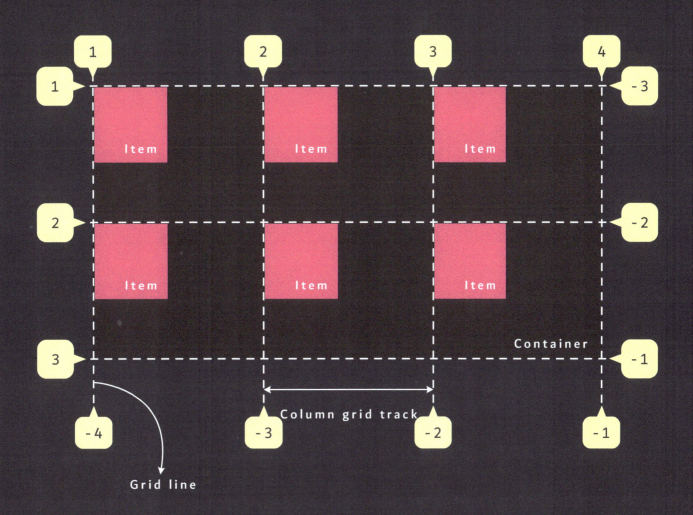

Grid Column Line

Grid column lines are the lines browsers create on a grid container's column (block) axis when you define the grid-template-columns property.

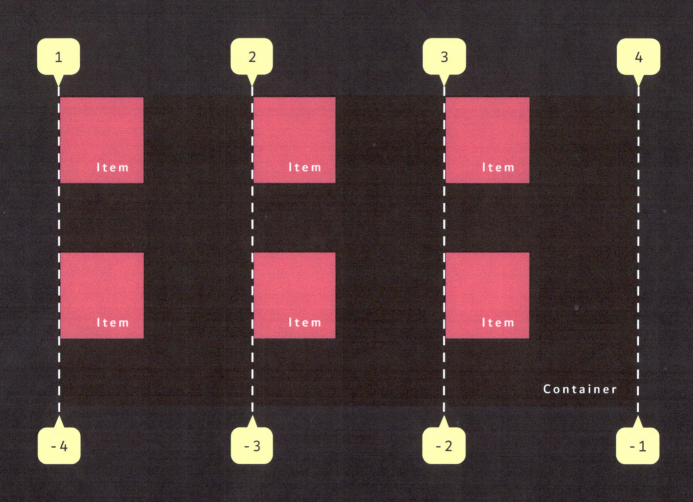

Grid Row Line

Grid row lines are the lines browsers create on a grid container's row (inline) axis when you define the grid-template-rows property.

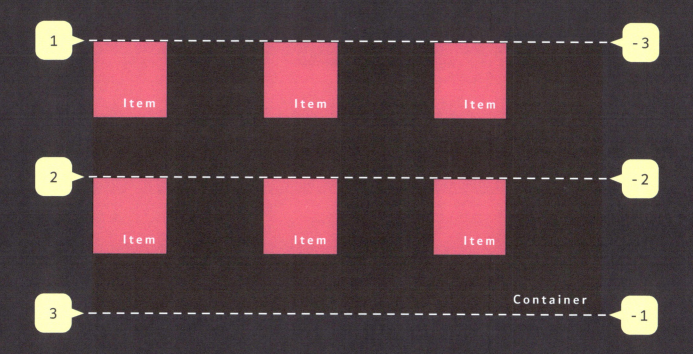

@oluwatobiss

@codesweetly

codesweetly.com

Other CodeSweetly Books...

The CSS Grid Guidebook

Available at Amazon
(https://amzn.to/3NgjPm3)

CSS Flexbox: Complete Guide

Available at Amazon
(https://amzn.to/3oPyonZ)

Visual Flexbox: Quick Guide

Available at Amazon
(https://amzn.to/44kLI2u)

CodeSweetly Sketchbook

Available at Amazon
(https://amzn.to/42kesah)

React Explained Clearly

Available at Amazon
(https://amzn.to/3HlCQzL)

C<8>DESWEETLY

CodeSweetly exists specifically to help make coding so easy and fun to learn.

Visit codesweetly.com to learn web technology topics with simplified articles, images, and cheat sheets.

www.ingramcontent.com/pod-product-compliance
Lightning Source LLC
LaVergne TN
LVHW060201050326
832903LV00016B/342